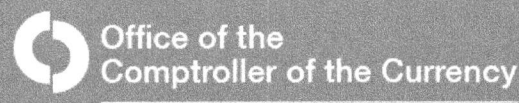

Office of the Comptroller of the Currency

Washington, DC 20219

Office *of the* Comptroller *of the* Currency

Director's Toolkit

DETECTING

RED FLAGS

IN BOARD REPORTS

A GUIDE
FOR DIRECTORS

February 2004
(reprint, September 2013)

DETECTING
RED FLAGS
IN BOARD REPORTS
A GUIDE
FOR DIRECTORS

Office of the Comptroller of the Currency

Washington, D.C.

Contents

I. Introduction

Good decisions begin with good information. A bank's board of directors needs concise, accurate, and timely reports to help it perform its fiduciary responsibilities. This booklet describes information generally found in board reports, and it highlights "red flags"—ratios or trends that may signal existing or potential problems. An effective board is alert for the appearance of red flags that give rise to further inquiry. By making further inquiry, the directors can determine if a substantial problem exists or may be forming.

This booklet supplements other OCC publications including the *Director's Book: The Role of a National Bank Director* and topical booklets in the *Comptroller's Handbook* series. While it describes information generally found in board reports, the guidance in this booklet does not constitute a legal opinion that conduct consistent with it protects a director from liability.

As discussed in the *Director's Book*, the board of directors must oversee the bank's operations to ensure that the bank operates in a safe and sound manner and that risks to the institution are properly controlled. The board's responsibilities include keeping informed of the bank's operating environment, hiring and retaining competent management, maintaining an appropriate board structure, establishing strategic plans, monitoring operations, overseeing business performance, reviewing and approving major corporate actions, and ensuring that the bank serves its community's credit needs. The board of directors also establishes policies in major areas, holds management accountable for implementing those policies, and ensures that risks to the institution are properly managed.

The financial services industry is changing rapidly, and the nature of risk taking is increasing in complexity and magnitude. Because of today's more complex business environment, directors must understand and assess the existing, potential, and prospective impact of risk positions on future bank performance. Managing risk prospectively means identifying it, measuring it accurately, understanding its implications, and ensuring that appropriate risk management, control, and reporting systems are in place before the risks lead to problems for the bank.

From a regulatory perspective, risk is the potential that events, expected or unanticipated, may have an adverse impact on the bank's capital or earnings. To control risk and mitigate its impact on the bank's financial performance, all banks must have risk management systems that identify, measure, control, and monitor risks. Strong risk management systems are particularly important when introducing new products or services, when the bank experiences strong growth, or during difficult economic times when loan officers may be inclined to take additional risks.

The OCC has defined nine categories of risk for bank supervision purposes. These nine risks are credit, liquidity, interest rate, price, foreign currency translation, compliance, strategic, reputation, and transaction. These risks are not mutually exclusive; any product or service may expose the bank to multiple risks.[1]

Because market conditions and organizational structures vary, there is no single risk management system that works in all banks. The board of directors must take steps to ensure that its risk management system is tailored to its specific needs and circumstances. Effective risk management requires an informed board, capable management, and appropriate staffing. The board uses management reports and other information systems to stay well informed and to assess risk within an institution. Board decisions based upon ineffective, inaccurate, or incomplete reporting may increase risk within the bank.

Subscribers to OCC BankNet[2] have access to analytical tools that allow directors to compare a bank's performance to a custom peer group and established benchmarks. Custom peer group information is available to national banks through

---

[1] For a more complete discussion of these risks, refer to the "Bank Supervision Process" booklet of the *Comptroller's Handbook*, available at www.occ.gov/static/publications/handbook/banksup.pdf.

[2] OCC BankNet is available exclusively to national banks and is located at http://www.nationalbanknet.gov.

the Comparative Analysis Reporting system (CAR)[3], and the Canary[4] system shows the financial performance of a bank against established benchmarks. Subscribers to BankNet use the CAR system to analyze their bank's financial performance and compare it to the performance of the peer group selected. The Canary benchmarks highlight leading indicators of increased risk. OCC established benchmarks for specific financial ratios at levels "typical" for the average community bank. To the extent a bank exceeds a number of these benchmarks, it may be experiencing levels of risk above "typical" levels. The Canary benchmarks help directors to understand their bank's risk profile and anticipate areas that could require stronger risk controls.

Although the board may depend on management's expertise to run daily operations, the board remains ultimately responsible for monitoring the bank's operations and levels of risk. The board can monitor the operations of the bank through management reports, but it must do more than merely accept and review these reports; it must be confident of their accuracy and reliability. Directors should ensure that management provides adequate and timely financial and performance information that can answer questions, such as:

- Is the bank's strategic plan realistic for the bank's circumstances?

- Is management meeting the goals established in the planning process? If no, why?

- Is the level of earnings consistent or erratic?

- Do earnings result from the implementation of planned bank strategies, or from transactions that, while increasing short-term earnings, raise longer term risk?

- Do audit programs test internal controls to identify inaccurate, incomplete, or unauthorized transactions; deficiencies in the safeguarding of assets; unreliable financial and regulatory

---

[3] Comparative Analysis Reporting (CAR) provides access to selected financial data for more than 8,700 institutions, including commercial banks and FDIC-insured savings banks.

[4] Canary is an early warning system that identifies banks that have the highest financial risk positions. Subscribers to BankNet may access the Canary reports of their own banks.

reporting; violations of law and regulations; and deviations from the institution's policies and procedures?

- Are policies and procedures in place that safeguard against conflicts of interest, insider fraud and abuses, and affiliate abuse?
- Is the bank giving due consideration to changes in external conditions?
- Is the bank being compensated adequately for the risks it is taking in its various product lines and activities?
- Does the bank have sufficient capital to support its risk profile and business strategies?
- Are financial reports and statements accurate, or do they reflect an incomplete evaluation of the bank's financial condition?
- Are the bank's goals and plans consistent with the directors' tolerance for risk?

To assist boards of directors in assessing risk prospectively, this booklet identifies various leading indicators of increasing credit risk, liquidity risk, and interest rate risk that should be a part of ongoing board reports. Other reports and performance measures outlined in this booklet are useful to directors in assessing the bank's current condition. This booklet is structured according to the types of information directors should receive. They should regularly receive reports on:

- Financial performance.
- Credit risk management.
- Liquidity risk management.
- Interest rate risk management.
- Investment portfolio management.
- Financial derivatives and off-balance-sheet activities.
- Audits and internal control.
- Consumer compliance.
- Asset management.
- Management information systems.
- Internet banking.
- OCC's overall assessment.

II. Reports Directors Should Receive Regularly

A. Financial Performance

Reports of financial performance should help directors assess the bank's condition; determine whether the level of risk taken by the bank conforms to the board's policies; and identify red flags. To use financial information effectively, directors should look at the trend and level of individual measures and the interrelationships among capital, asset quality, earnings, liquidity, market risk, and balance sheet growth. Financial reports should focus on comparative financial statements and key financial performance ratios and highlight areas of key risks.

Comparative financial statements include:

- Income statements for the month and year-to-date, which are compared with the budget, with results from prior years, and with projections, if appropriate.

- Balance sheets, which compare balances in individual asset and liability categories with balances at the same date in the previous month, the previous year, and with projections, if appropriate.

In reviewing these items, directors should identify any item that has changed significantly or that varies significantly from the budget, generally 10 percent or more, and should ask management to explain the deviation.

Directors should regularly receive and review reports from management that contain key financial performance ratios and trends that facilitate effective monitoring of risk and financial performance. Many such ratios, including those referred to in the following paragraphs, may be found in the quarterly Uniform Bank Performance Report (UBPR), and others can be computed from internal bank records. The UBPR, which is computer generated from bank call report data and is available at the FFIEC Web site (http://www.ffiec.gov/), contains both historical and peer group information. (A bank's peer group includes banks of similar size, type, and location.) The UBPR can help directors evaluate a bank's current condition, trends in financial performance, and comparisons with its peer group.[5] Directors should determine the reason for significant variances in the bank's performance when compared with the peer group.

1. Capital

Capital is the cushion that protects banks and their customers and shareholders against loss resulting from the assumption of risk. As a result, the adequacy of capital is very closely related to the individual risk profile of each bank. Overall capital adequacy of a bank is measured both quantitatively and qualitatively. The quantitative analysis focuses on risk-based and leverage ratios. The qualitative assessment considers the quality and level of earnings, the quality of assets, the bank's business strategy, the effectiveness of risk management, and management's overall ability to identify, measure, monitor, and control risk.

The board and management must determine how much capital the bank should hold. This determination may change over time based on the risk inherent in the bank's business profile, dividend expectations of the bank's shareholders, economic variables that affect the bank's market or customer base, and other factors. Although banks must maintain minimum capital ratios established in risk-based capital guidelines (12 CFR 3), most banks are expected to maintain capital ratios higher than the required minimums.

Adequate capital supports future growth, fosters public confidence in the bank's condition, provides the capacity under the bank's legal lending limit to serve customers' needs, and protects the bank from unexpected losses. Directors should monitor the following ratios to help ensure compliance with

---

[5] Custom peer group information is available to national banks through the Comparative Analysis Reporting system (CAR) on OCC's National BankNet.

regulatory minimum requirements. These ratios are widely used and can also be found on the UBPR, CAR, or Canary.

- Tier 1 capital/adjusted average assets—the amount of capital supporting the bank's loans and other assets. Tier 1 capital includes the purest and most stable forms of capital. This ratio is commonly called the leverage ratio.

- Tier 1 capital/risk-weighted assets (tier 1 risk-based ratio) and total capital/risk-weighted assets (total risk-based ratio)—the amount of capital in relation to the amount of credit risk associated with assets on and off the balance sheet. Total capital adds limited amounts of other capital to the tier 1 level.

The ratios below may be useful in evaluating the bank's ongoing ability to maintain sufficient capital levels.

- Cash dividends/net income—the percentage of net income paid out to shareholders in dividends.

- Equity growth rate versus asset growth rate—measures the extent to which capital growth is keeping pace with asset growth.

All insured depository institutions are subject to the prompt corrective action (PCA) framework outlined in 12 CFR 6.4. Although minimum regulatory capital standards can generally be satisfied at the "adequately capitalized" level, most banks strive to maintain a "well capitalized" status under the PCA framework. A bank is "well capitalized" if:

- Its leverage ratio is at least 5 percent.

- Its tier 1 risk-based ratio is at least 6 percent.

- Its total risk-based ratio is at least 10 percent.

- It is not subject to any written agreement, order, capital directive, or prompt corrective action directive to maintain a specific capital level for any capital measure.

A bank is subject to certain restrictions that increase in severity as the PCA capital category of the bank deteriorates. These restrictions begin to apply when a bank falls below "well capitalized." For example, an adequately capitalized bank must apply for and receive a waiver from the Federal Deposit Insurance Corporation (FDIC) before it can accept, renew, or roll over brokered deposits. Banks in any of the three "undercapitalized" categories of PCA are not in compliance with the minimum regulatory requirements and are subject to a range of additional supervisory restrictions and requirements.[6] Complete information on the PCA capital categories is published at 12 CFR 6.4.

Financial Performance—Capital Red Flags:

- Ratios below "well capitalized" or those required by order or agreement.

- Capital growth rate is less than total asset growth rate.

- Ratios significantly different from peer ratios.

- Declining capital levels or ratios.

- Dividend payout ratio is significantly higher than peer ratios.

- Concentration in nontraditional activities.

- Significant growth in off-balance-sheet activities.

---

[6] The three "undercapitalized" categories of PCA are undercapitalized, significantly undercapitalized, and critically undercapitalized.

2. Asset Quality

Asset quality is a function of the quantity of existing and potential credit risk associated with the loan and investment portfolios, other real estate owned, other assets, and off-balance-sheet transactions. Management maintains asset quality by identifying, measuring, monitoring, and controlling credit risk. Directors should ensure the existence of adequate underwriting and risk selection standards, sound credit administration practices, and appropriate risk identification practices.

When evaluating asset quality, directors should consider the adequacy of the allowance for loan and lease losses (ALLL); the level, distribution, severity, and trend of problem, classified, nonaccrual, restructured, delinquent, and nonperforming assets; the existence of concentrations of credit; credit risk arising from off-balance-sheet transactions; loan growth; and the volume and nature of credit policy and documentation exceptions.

In addition to reviewing reports prepared by management, directors should regularly review the following credit risk and asset quality leading indicators for signs of increasing credit risk. These indicators are widely used and can also be found on UBPR, CAR, or Canary.

- Loan growth—measures the rate of growth in total loans and leases. Rapid growth, particularly as measured against local, regional, and national economic indicators, has long been associated with subsequent credit quality problems.

- Loans to equity—measures the multiple of bank equity capital invested in loans. All other factors held equal, as this ratio increases, so does risk to bank capital from credit risk. When this ratio is high, bank capital may be disproportionately affected by events that have an adverse impact on credit quality.

- Change in portfolio mix—measures the change in the composition of the portfolio over a given time frame. Changes in portfolio mix may indicate increasing risk, or decreasing risk. The larger the change the greater the reasons to investigate its effect on the credit risk profile.

- Loans to assets—measures the percentage of the bank's total assets that are invested in loans. As this percentage increases, credit risk may also increase.

- Loan yield—measures the yield on the loan portfolio. The yield on the loan portfolio should reflect the risk of default and loss in the underlying loans as well as risks in the portfolio. High yields may indicate higher credit risk.

- Noncurrent loans and leases/total loans and leases—the percentage of the loan portfolio not performing as agreed (i.e., loans and leases 90 days or more past due plus loans and leases not accruing interest). This measure is also referred to as nonperforming loans.

- Noncurrent loans and leases/equity capital—the percentage of the bank's permanent capital base threatened by noncurrent loans. The calculation for this ratio may include the ALLL in the denominator because the ALLL is available to absorb loan losses without reducing capital.

- ALLL/total loans and leases—the percentage of total loans the bank has set aside (reserved) to cover possible losses in the loan portfolio.

- ALLL/net loan and lease losses—the number of times the existing loan loss reserve would be able to cover the bank's losses during a given period.

- Noncurrent loans and leases/ALLL—the percentage of the loan loss reserve that is available to absorb losses on noncurrent loans.

- Net loan and lease losses/average loans and leases—the percentage of the loan portfolio charged off during the period.

Financial Performance—Asset Quality and Credit Risk Red Flags:

- Significant increase in loans to total assets ratio.

- Significant increase in loans to equity ratio.

- Significant change in portfolio mix.

- Significant upward or downward trend in the percent of the ALLL to total loans and leases.

- High growth rates in total loans or within individual categories of loans.

- Significant increase in loan yields.

- Loan yields significantly higher than peer group.

- Downward trends in risk ratings among pass credits and/or increases in special mention or classified assets.

- Significant volume of retail loans that have been extended, deferred, renewed, or rewritten.

- Increasing levels of past-due and nonperforming loans as a percent of loans.

- Significant changes in the ALLL.

- Significant increases in ALLL provisions.

- Stable or declining ALLL at the same time net loan losses trend upward.

- Annual net charge-offs that exceed the balance in the ALLL.

- ALLL averages and percentages significantly different from the peer group's.

- Increasing levels of other real estate owned.

- Loans identified by internal and external loan review that are not included in problem loan lists provided by management.

- Any significant changes in the above relative to historical performance, planned performance, or peer performance.

3. Earnings

The directors' review of earnings should focus on the quantity, trend, and sustainability or quality of earnings. A bank with good earnings performance can expand, remain competitive, augment its capital funds, and, at the same time, provide a return to shareholders through dividends. When a bank's quantity or quality of earnings diminishes, the cause is usually either excessive or inadequately managed credit risk or high levels of interest rate risk. High credit risk, which often requires the bank to add to its ALLL, may result in an elevated level of loan losses, while high interest rate risk may increase the volatility of an institution's earnings from interest rate changes. The quality of earnings may also be diminished by undue reliance on extraordinary gains, nonrecurring events, or favorable tax effects. Future earnings may be affected adversely by an inability to forecast or control funding and operating expenses, improperly executed or ill-advised business strategies, or poorly managed or uncontrolled exposure to other risks.

The level and trend of the following measures, compared with the bank's previous performance and the current performance of peer banks, are important in evaluating earnings. These measures are widely used and can also be found on the UBPR, CAR, or Canary.

- Net income/average assets—how efficiently the bank's assets generate earnings. This ratio, commonly referred to as return on average assets (ROAA), is a primary indicator of profitability.

- Net income/average total equity—the rate of return on the shareholders' investment. This ratio is commonly referred to as return on equity (ROE).

- Net interest income/average earning assets—the difference between interest earned (on loans, leases, federal funds, investments, etc.) and interest paid (for deposits, federal funds, borrowings, etc.) compared with average earning assets. This ratio is commonly referred to as the net interest margin (NIM). Net interest income historically has been most banks' largest source of earnings. Directors also look at the components of interest income and expense to identify changes in volume and spreads.

- Noninterest income/average assets—bank reliance on income derived from bank services and sources other than interest-bearing assets. Directors should review sources and volatility of and significant changes in noninterest income.

- Overhead (noninterest) expense/average assets—efficiency of the bank's operations. Although controlling overhead expense is important, directors should be alert for too much cost cutting, e.g., reducing staff below prudent levels and forgoing information systems upgrades. Such decisions may expose the bank to significant risks that could impair future earnings.

- Provision expense/average assets—the relative cost of adding to the loan loss reserve. Loan losses erode capital and reduce earnings. The loan report to the board should describe how various loan loss scenarios might affect earnings. For more about the loan report, see the "Credit Portfolio Management" section of this booklet.

Financial Performance—Earnings Red Flags:

- Significant increases or decreases in noninterest income.

- Significantly higher or lower average personnel expenses than peer banks.

- Significant variances in the ROAA, ROE, or NIM from prior periods and as compared with peer group.

- Significant variances from budgeted amounts on income or expense items and balance sheet accounts.

---

4. Liquidity

When evaluating liquidity, directors should compare the bank's current level of liquidity, plus liquidity that would likely be available from other sources, with its funding needs to determine whether the bank's funds management practices are adequate. Bank management should be able to manage unplanned changes in funding sources, and react to changes in market conditions that could hinder the bank's ability to liquidate assets quickly with minimal loss. Funds management practices should ensure that the bank does not maintain liquidity at too high a cost or rely unduly on wholesale or credit-sensitive funding sources. These funding sources may not be available in times of financial stress or when market conditions are adverse. Banks should maintain an adequate level of liquid assets and a stable base of deposits and other funding sources.

Refer to Section C of this booklet for liquidity leading indicators that directors should regularly review for signs of increasing liquidity risk.

Financial Performance—Liquidity Red Flags:

- Significant increases in reliance on wholesale funding.

- Significant increases in large certificates of deposit, brokered deposits, or deposits with interest rates higher than the market.

- Significant increases in borrowings.

- Significant increases in dependence on funding sources other than core deposits.

- Declines in levels of core deposits.

- Significant decreases in short-term investments.

---

5. Sensitivity to Market Risk

To assess the bank's market risk, directors determine how changes in interest rates, foreign exchange rates, commodity prices, or equity prices could reduce the bank's earnings or capital. The primary source of market risk for many banks is interest rate risk, i.e., the sensitivity to changes in interest rates. Foreign operations and trading activities in some larger institutions can be a significant source of market risk.

Refer to Section D for ratios that can help directors evaluate the bank's sensitivity to changes in interest rates.

Financial Performance—Interest Rate Risk Red Flags:

- Capital falling below the level established by the board to support interest rate risk.

- Significant increases or decreases in the percent of long-term assets to total assets.

- Significant decrease in the percent of nonmaturity funding sources to long-term assets.

- High or increasing percent of asset depreciation to tier 1 capital.

---

6. Growth

Directors should also look at the effect of growth on the bank's exposure to risk in key categories, such as asset quality, earnings, capital, and liquidity. Rapid growth may harm the bank. Managing additional risk or a new risk profile can be costly and can strain resources. In a growth environment, personnel with the requisite expertise should handle the new lines of business or assume additional responsibility. The bank must also have control and information systems that adequately handle the bank's increase in size and its greater exposure to risk.

Directors should identify growth patterns by comparing historical and budgeted growth rates for assets, capital, loans, volatile liabilities, core deposits, and income and expenses. Comparing the bank's growth rates with those of its peers may also indicate whether the bank is growing inordinately.

Financial Performance—Growth Red Flags:

- Growth that is inconsistent with the bank's budget or strategic plan.

- Growth that is significantly greater than that of peer banks, even if projected in the bank's budget or strategic plan.

- Growth that is unaccompanied by an increasing level of and sophistication in risk management controls.

- Growth that results in a higher risk profile than forecast.

- Declining capital levels or ratios that result from asset growth.

- Reliance on unstable or short-term funding sources to support growth.

- Introduction of new products or activities with little or no expertise or inadequate risk management controls.

- Growth that is generated largely by brokered or agent transactions.

B. Credit Portfolio Management

Boards that effectively oversee the loan portfolio understand and control the bank's risk profile and its credit culture. Directors accomplish this by having a thorough knowledge of the portfolio's composition and its inherent risks. The directors should understand the portfolio's industry and geographic concentrations, average risk ratings, and other credit risk characteristics. They should also ensure that the bank has appropriate staffing and expertise for all of its lending activities and that management is capable of effectively managing the risks being assumed.[7]

Directors should monitor adverse trends in the loan portfolio and should judge the adequacy of the allowance for loan and lease losses (ALLL) by reviewing the loan reports. The board, or a loan committee of directors, should receive information on new and renewed loans that represent large single-borrower exposures, material participations purchased and sold, past-due and nonperforming loans, other real estate owned (OREO), problem loans and trends in risk ratings identified by management and examiners, charge-offs and recoveries, management's analyses of the adequacy of the ALLL, composition of the loan portfolio, concentrations of credit, credit and collateral exceptions, and customers with large total borrowings. Comparative and trend data are usually best presented in graph form.

1. Credit Quality

Normally, the most readily available information for directors about credit quality comes from management's internal risk rating reports, reports on past-due and nonaccrual loans, renegotiated and restructured loan reports, and policy exception reports. Reviewing these reports can help directors identify negative trends early.

---

[7] See the "Loan Portfolio Management" booklet of the *Comptroller's Handbook* for additional information on loan portfolio management, available at www.occ.gov/static/publications/handbook/lpm.pdf.

Directors review the following reports to assess loan quality.

- Risk rating reports—summarize the total dollar amount of loans in each risk rating category, often by division or product. These reports are especially useful for monitoring risk-rating trends. In addition to the problem loan categories, the OCC strongly encourages banks to develop multiple pass (non-problem) rating grades so that negative trends in overall loan quality can be identified more quickly.

- Problem loan reports—identify problem or watch credits and quantify the bank's potential loss on each significant problem credit. The bank's internal loan classifications should be updated and summarized periodically and should be easily translatable to the OCC classification system (pass, special mention, substandard, doubtful, and loss). Directors must understand why a loan is a problem and what action management is taking to correct the situation.

- Rating migration reports—show how loan ratings have changed over time. At a base date, each loan is categorized by risk rating, with ratings periodically updated (generally quarterly). This format enables directors to observe changes in the risk ratings and provides a view of portfolio quality over time. Directors should understand when loan quality deteriorates and what actions management is taking to correct the situation.

- Past-due and nonaccrual reports—show seriously delinquent borrowers and tell the percent of loans past due by loan category (i.e., commercial, installment, real estate). Directors should understand the reasons for delinquencies.

- Renegotiated and restructured loan reports—identify loans whose original terms or structure have been modified, usually due to financial stress of the borrower. High levels of problem loans that were brought current by renegotiating or restructuring the terms, or repeated extensions in the case of a single credit, can signal an effort to mask the true quality of the loan portfolio. Directors should understand why loans were restructured or renegotiated.

- OREO reports—detail efforts to dispose of each piece of other real estate owned (generally foreclosed properties) and show if appraisals are current for all parcels.

- Exception reports—list exceptions to loan policies, procedures, and underwriting standards. The reports should include the trend in number and dollar amount of loans approved that are exceptions to policy as well as the percentage of loans that are exceptions to policy. Directors require that management explain these exceptions and determine whether to re-enforce or revise loan policies.

- Concentration reports—show lending concentrations by type of loan, regions, etc.

2. Allowance for Loan and Lease Losses

The allowance for loan and lease losses is a valuation reserve charged against the bank's operating income. Directors should ensure that provisions are reasonable and that the allowance covers all estimated inherent loan and lease losses.[8]

Directors should review the following information to determine whether the ALLL is adequate:

- Management's quarterly evaluation of the adequacy of the ALLL prepared as of call report dates.

- Management's problem loan list.

- Charge-off and recovery experience.

- A reconcilement of the ALLL for the current period and previous year-end.

- Any independent analysis of the ALLL (e.g., external loan review).

---

[8] See the "Allowance for Loan and Lease Losses" booklet of the *Comptroller's Handbook* for additional information on the valuation reserve, available at www.occ.gov/static/publications/handbook/alll.pdf.

3. Credit Summary

Board members can find out what types of loans the bank is making and management's lending practices by looking at lists of new credits approved, loans renewed, concentrations of credit, and participations purchased and sold. Management and the board together should establish dollar limits for the loans detailed in those reports.

Credit Portfolio Red Flags:

- Significant shifts in the bank's risk rating profile or increase in the number or dollar amount of problem or watch loans as a percent of loans, in aggregate, or for loan types.

- Large or increasing volume of loans granted or renewed with policy exceptions.

- Large or increasing volume of credit/collateral exceptions.

- Rapid growth in total loan volume or particular types of lending.

- Loans remaining on the problem loan list for extended periods of time without resolution.

- Loan review personnel reporting to a person(s) other than the board, a board committee, or a unit independent of the lending function.

- Delinquent internal loan reviews or late identification of problem loans.

- Change in scope and frequency of internal loan reviews.

- Large concentrations of credit.

- Loans to directors, significant shareholders, management, other insiders, and third parties performing services for the bank, external accountants, auditors, and marketing firms.

- Loans to affiliates.

- Excessive out-of-territory lending.

- Excessive reliance on third-party loan brokers or service providers.

- Borrowers on the overdraft or uncollected funds reports.

- Growth in the ALLL that is significantly greater or less than the percentage growth in total loans over a given period.

- Nonperforming or problem loans as a percentage of total loans increasing at a rate greater than the ALLL.

- Loan officer compensation tied solely to growth or volume targets (i.e., without credit quality attributes).

- Insufficient controls when purchasing loans.

C. Liquidity Risk Management

The board and senior management are responsible for understanding the nature and level of liquidity risk assumed by the bank and the tools used to manage that risk. The board and senior management should also ensure that the bank's funding strategy and its implementation are consistent with their expressed risk tolerance.[9]

The board of directors' primary duties in this area should include establishing and guiding the bank's strategic direction and tolerance for liquidity risk; selecting senior managers who will have the authority and responsibility to manage liquidity risk; monitoring the bank's performance and overall liquidity risk profile; and ensuring that liquidity risk is identified, measured, monitored, and controlled.

While there is rarely a single liquidity risk measurement that fully quantifies the amount of risk assumed, directors should review regularly a complement of measurement tools, including forward-looking risk measures. Forward-looking measurement tools project future funding needs for tomorrow, next month, and six months from now, and so on. Traditional static liquidity measurements provide only limited insight into the management of day-to-day liquidity. Bank managers must have a comprehensive understanding of the cash flow characteristics of their institution's on- and off-balance-sheet activities to manage liquidity levels prudently over time. When reasonable assumptions are used, this provides a sound basis for liquidity planning.

The following reports should assist directors in assessing the bank's liquidity risk:

- Liquidity risk report—shows the level and trend of the bank or banking company's liquidity risk by a variety of appropriate measures. The report should indicate how much liquidity risk the bank is assuming, whether management is complying with risk limits, and whether management's

---

[9] See the "Liquidity" booklet of the *Comptroller's Handbook* for additional information on liquidity risk management, available at www.occ.gov/static/publications/handbook/liquidity.pdf.

strategies are consistent with the board's expressed risk tolerance.

- Funds provider report—lists large funds providers and identifies funding concentrations. These reports should include consolidated information from all commonly owned banks.

- Projected needs and sources—projects future liquidity needs for a prescribed timeframe and compares these projections to the sources of funds available.

- Funds availability report—states the amount of borrowing capacity remaining under established lines of credit. This report indicates the amount of funding the bank can realize given its financial condition and qualifying collateral.

- Cash flow or funding gap report— reflects the quantity of cash available within each of a series of selected time periods compared to the quantity of cash required within the same time period. The difference between the available and required amounts is the cash flow or funding "gap." If the bank plans for an increased volume of business or has optionality in its assets, liabilities or both, a dynamic cash flow or funding gap report is the better practice. A dynamic report incorporates growth projections and the impact of rate changes on cash flows derived from assets and liabilities with explicit and embedded call features.

- Funding concentration report reflects significant funding from a single source (FHLB, jumbo CDs, etc.) or from multiple sources possessing common credit or rate sensitivity. A funding concentration exists when a single decision or factor could cause a significant and sudden withdrawal of funds. The dollar amount of a funding concentration is an amount that, if withdrawn, alone or at the same time as a few other large accounts, would cause the bank to change its day-to-day funding strategy significantly.

- Contingency Funding Plan (CFP)—may incorporate the funding gap report or be considered an outgrowth of it. The CFP forecasts funding needs and funding sources (and therefore gap) under varying market scenarios resulting in rapid liability erosion (usually because of increasing customer concerns about the asset quality of the bank), or excessive asset growth (for example, because of early amortization of securitizations).

The following ratios can also be useful as liquidity risk indicators. These ratios are widely used and can also be found on the UBPR, CAR, or Canary. Adverse changes in these leading indicators could indicate increasing liquidity risk.

- Loan to Deposit Ratio—indicates the extent to which a bank's deposit structure funds the loan portfolio. The higher the ratio the more reliance that a bank has on non-deposit sources to fund the loan portfolio.

- Net non-core funding dependence—calculated by subtracting short-term investments from non-core liabilities and dividing the resulting difference by long-term assets. This ratio indicates the degree of reliance on funds from the professional money markets to fund earning assets. Professional markets are credit and price sensitive. These funds will move out of the bank in the event of real or perceived asset quality or other fundamental problems at the bank.

- Net short-term liabilities/total assets—calculated by taking the difference in short-term assets from short-term liabilities and dividing by total assets. The ratio indicates the degree of exposure assumed by funding assets with short-term liabilities, also referred to as rollover risk. Generally, the higher the number, the more vulnerable the bank is to funding sources rolling out. This requires the bank to find new funding sources for existing assets.

- On-hand liquidity/total liabilities—calculated by dividing net liquid assets by total liabilities. This ratio measures the bank's ability to meet liquidity needs from on-hand liquid assets. The lower the ratio the greater the likelihood that the bank will need to use market funding sources to meet incremental liquidity needs.

- Reliance on wholesale funding—calculated by dividing all wholesale funding by total funding. This measures the portion of the bank's total funds that are from wholesale sources. Banks with high volumes of wholesale funding should make sure that they have up-to-date contingency funding plans.

Liquidity Risk Red Flags:

- Liquidity risk that exceeds risk limits established by the board.

- A negative trend or significantly increased risk in any area or product line, particularly a decline in indicators of asset quality or in earnings performance or projections.

- Funding concentration from a single source or multiple sources with a common credit or rate sensitivity.

- Rapid asset growth funded by rate and/or credit sensitive funding, such as borrowed funds, brokered deposits, national market certificates of deposit, or deposits obtained through CD listing services.

- Increased funding costs because of customer or counterparty concerns about increasing risk.

- Eliminated or decreased credit line availability from lenders, including correspondent banks.

- Larger purchases in the brokered funds or other potentially volatile markets.

- Mismatched funding—funding long-term assets with short-term liabilities or funding sources containing embedded options.

- Frequent exceptions to the bank's liquidity risk policy.

- Absence of an effective Contingency Funding Plan that is current and commensurate with the complexity of the bank's funding activities.

- Change in significant funding sources.

D. Interest Rate Risk Management

An effective board understands the nature and level of the bank's interest rate risk, determines whether that risk is consistent with the bank's overall strategies, and assesses whether the bank's methods of managing interest rate risk are appropriate. The directors establish the bank's tolerance for interest rate risk and monitor its performance and overall interest rate risk profile. The directors also ensure that the level of interest rate risk is maintained at prudent levels and is supported by adequate capital. Thus, the board considers the bank's exposure to current and potential interest rate risk. Directors also assess the bank's exposure to other risks, such as credit, liquidity, and transaction.

Accurate and timely measurement of interest rate risk is necessary for proper risk management and control. The risk measurement system should identify and quantify the major sources of the bank's interest rate exposure. The board should request and review reports that measure the bank's current interest rate risk position relative to earnings at risk and capital at risk limits.[10] The three most common risk measurement systems used to quantify a bank's interest rate risk exposure are gap reports, simulation models, and economic value sensitivity models. They should be requested and reviewed by the board.

- Gap reports—calculate the difference between rate-sensitive assets and rate-sensitive liabilities at various intervals or time periods. The gap at the one-year level can be used to calculate the amount of net interest income at risk. Gap reports generally are used to evaluate how a bank's net interest income will be affected by a change in interest rates.

- Simulation models—measure interest rate risk arising from current and future business scenarios. Earnings simulation models evaluate risk exposure over a period of time, taking into account projected changes in balance sheet structures, pricing, maturity relationships, and assumptions about new

---

[10] See the "Interest Rate Risk" booklet of the *Comptroller's Handbook* for additional information on these risk limits, available at www.occ.gov/static/publications/handbook/irr.pdf.

business and growth. Reports generally show future balance sheet and income statements under a number of interest rate and business-mix scenarios.

- Economic value sensitivity models— capture the interest rate risk of the bank's business mix across the spectrum of maturities. These models generally compute the present value of the bank's assets, liabilities, and off-balance-sheet accounts under alternative interest rate scenarios and the sensitivity of that value to changes in interest rates.

All national banks should measure earnings at risk due to changes in interest rates. Well-managed banks with meaningful exposure to longer term or options risk should augment their earnings at risk measures with systems that quantify the potential effect of changes in interest rates on their economic value of equity. These systems are appropriate for banks with significant exposure to longer term assets, embedded options, and off-balance-sheet activities.

The following ratios can be useful as interest rate risk indicators. They are widely used and can also be found on the UBPR, CAR, or Canary. Adverse changes in these indicators could indicate increasing interest rate risk.

- Long-term assets/total assets—commonly used as an indicator of repricing risk. A higher ratio generally suggests that a bank has a sizeable amount of assets that cannot be repriced for a long period of time. Those assets will lose value and will depreciate if interest rates rise, because they will be paying lower yields relative to prevailing market rates.

- Nonmaturity deposits/long-term assets—estimates the degree that nonmaturity funding sources cover long-term assets on the balance sheet. Such sources include demand deposit accounts (DDA), money market demand accounts (MMDA), and savings and NOW accounts. Banks with high ratios should be less vulnerable to increases in interest rates.

- Residential real estate /total assets—indicates the magnitude of short options risk (also called negative convexity) in the balance sheet. Short options positions indicate that the bank has provided its customers with the option of either prepaying the asset when rates are low or not pre-paying when rates rise. Short options increase a bank's interest rate risk by compressing margins in both rising and falling rate environments.

- Asset depreciation/tier 1 capital—measures the proportion of capital offset by estimated depreciation in the available-for-sale and held-to-maturity investment portfolios, plus an estimate of potential depreciation in the residential loan portfolio. Depreciation in all these assets is usually the result of yields that are below market rate.

The following management reports should assist directors in assessing the bank's interest rate risk:

- Risk Summary—summary reports showing the level and trend of the bank or bank holding company's interest rate risk using a variety of appropriate measures. The report should indicate the amount of risk the bank is assuming, whether management is complying with board approved risk limits, and whether management's strategies are consistent with the board's expressed risk tolerance.

- Earnings at Risk—detail report showing projected changes in net interest income because of changes in interest rates under parallel and nonparallel interest rate changes.

- Audit Reports—periodic audits of interest rate risk measurement processes that assess the appropriateness of the risk measurement system, data integrity, reasonableness of assumptions, and validity of risk measurement calculations.

- Capital at Risk—detail report for economic value of equity at risk or other long-term risk measure.

- Net Interest Margin Analysis—analyzes the net interest margin and identifies the source(s) of material changes. This analysis isolates the effects of changes in interest rates, asset growth, and balance sheet restructuring on the net interest margin.

Interest Rate Risk Red Flags:

- Significant changes in net interest income.

- High or increasing volume of assets with embedded options, such as residential real estate mortgages, mortgage-backed securities, callable securities, mortgage servicing rights, residual assets, and structured notes.

- High or increasing volume of liabilities with embedded options, such as putable or convertible funding products or structured CDs.

- Adverse changes in the level and trends of aggregate interest rate risk exposure.

- Noncompliance with the board's established risk tolerance levels and limits.

- Lack of an independent review or audit of the interest rate risk management process.

- Absence of meaningful risk limits.

- Unauthorized or frequent exceptions to the interest rate risk policy.

- The inability of management to provide reports that identify and quantify the major sources of the bank's interest rate risk in a timely manner and describe assumptions used to determine interest rate risk.

E. Investment Portfolio Management

Banks may own investment securities and money market assets to manage asset and liability positions, diversify their earning assets base, maintain a liquidity cushion, and meet pledging requirements. The investment portfolio for most national banks constitutes a significant earning asset. The increasing complexity of the securities available in the marketplace has heightened the need for effective management of the portfolio. Oversight of investment portfolio activities is an important part of managing the bank's overall interest rate, liquidity, and credit risk profiles.

Directors play a key role in overseeing the bank's investment activities. They establish strategic direction and risk tolerance limits, review portfolio activity, assess risk profile, evaluate performance, and monitor management's compliance with authorized risk limits.[11]

1. Selection of Securities Dealers

Many banks rely on securities sales representatives and strategists to recommend investment strategies, and the timing and relative value of proposed securities transactions. Directors review and approve a list of securities firms with whom the bank is authorized to do business. Directors also provide management guidance on credit quality and other standards appropriate to ensure that dealers used by the bank are financially stable, reputable, and knowledgeable.

In managing a bank's relationship with securities dealers, the board of directors may want to consider prohibiting employees who purchase and sell securities for the bank from engaging in personal securities transactions with the same securities firms the bank uses for its transactions. Such a prohibition may reduce the risk of a conflict of interest for bank personnel.

---

[11] See "An Examiner's Guide to Investment Products and Practices" (December 1992) for additional discussions of fundamental bank investment policies, procedures, practices, controls, and investment product profiles.

2. Categorization of Securities

When a bank purchases a security, management must assign it to one of three accounting classifications. The classifications are held-to-maturity, available-for-sale, and trading. The choice depends upon how much managerial flexibility the bank wants to have. A held-to-maturity (HTM) security is one for which the bank has the intent and ability to hold the security to maturity. The bank may account for HTM securities at historical cost. With historical cost accounting, changes in market value do not affect earnings or the bank's reported capital. However, the bank sacrifices flexibility with the HTM designation, since it has stated its intent to hold the securities to maturity.

The available-for-sale (AFS) designation permits a bank to sell securities prior to maturity, for example, to take gains and/ or reposition the portfolio based upon management's outlook for interest rates. For accounting purposes, AFS securities are marked-to-market. Changes in the market value of AFS securities are reflected in "Other Comprehensive Income" (OCI), a separate component of capital. Value changes in AFS securities do not affect a bank's regulatory capital, but they do affect capital reported under generally accepted accounting principles (GAAP). Sale of an HTM security, for reasons other than credit and other limited "safe harbors," may call into question the appropriateness of the HTM designation for other securities and may result in a required reclassification to AFS and the use of mark-to-market, as opposed to historical cost, accounting for these securities. Trading securities are marked-to-market, with gains and losses reflected in the income statement.

Directors are ultimately responsible for effective oversight of a national bank's investment portfolio. However, a bank's board may delegate investment decision-making authority for all or a portion of its investment securities portfolio either to a nonaffiliated firm or to a person who is not an employee of the institution or one of its affiliates. Banks that hire outside portfolio managers hope to obtain more professional portfolio management, and earn higher total returns and incur lower transactions costs. The ability to use the HTM designation will depend upon the amount of discretion given to the outside manager. Most arrangements require the manager to obtain approval from the bank prior to executing a securities transaction. The bank could continue to classify securities as HTM if it retains the authority to approve the transaction. However, in the rare cases when a bank gives purchase and sale discretion to the outside manager, it will have to categorize securities under the manager's control as AFS.

3. Investment Reports

Reports must focus on risk, rather than merely report data, to provide effective supervision over investment activities. Directors may find the following reports helpful in assessing the overall quality, liquidity, and performance of the investment portfolio:

- Maturity breakdown, average maturity, and interest rate risk—shows the maturity and interest rate risk of each sector of the investment portfolio (Treasuries, agencies, corporates, municipals, etc.) and of the portfolio as a whole.

- Distribution of credit ratings (by a major rating service) for all municipal and corporate securities—shows the percent of the portfolio in each rating category. This report provides useful information on the overall credit quality of the portfolio.

- Adjusted historical cost for each security sector relative to its current market value—shows the cost and market values of HTM securities. For AFS securities, it shows the amount recorded as an unrealized gain or loss in Other Comprehensive Income.

- Purchases and sales—indicates the type of security, its par value, maturity date, rate, yield, cost and sales prices, and any profit or loss. For purchases, risk-focused information would reflect value sensitivity, i.e., how much the security's value would change for a specified change in market yields and any applicable policy limits. A pre-purchase analysis should identify such value sensitivity.

- Sensitivity analysis of the value of the portfolio in different interest rate environments—compares the value in each interest rate scenario with the current portfolio value, illustrating the amount of portfolio interest rate risk. This report also provides a means of ensuring that management has complied with the board's tolerance for risk.

Investment Portfolio Red Flags:

- Purchase of securities that do not meet board guidelines on risk or quality.

- Securities purchased without pre-purchase risk analysis.

- Absence of management's estimation of portfolio valuation sensitivities.

- Purchase of securities in excess of concentration limits.

- Purchase of securities with yields well above market levels (possible "yield chasing").

- Purchasing a relatively large amount of securities in a short time period.

- Frequent use of lending authority to acquire securities.

- Frequent policy exceptions.

- Use of one securities dealer for most, or all, securities purchases and sales.

- Investment purchases from securities dealers not approved by the board of directors.

- Sale of securities previously designated as HTM, or transfer of securities from HTM to AFS.

- The classification of securities with high value sensitivity as HTM.

- Large volumes of non-rated, below-investment-grade (lower than BBB or Baa), or out-of-area bonds (may indicate a credit quality problem).

- Exclusive reliance on rating agencies' ratings for nongovernment securities.

- Investment yields that are well above or below the market or peer group average.

- Significant changes in the type, quality, or maturity distribution of the portfolio.

- Significant deterioration in the market value of investments.

- Absence of credit risk assessment for safekeeping agent.

F. Financial Derivatives and Off-Balance-Sheet Activities

Banks are increasingly using financial derivatives and other off-balance-sheet transactions, such as securitization activities, to manage financial risk and increase income. The broad categories of risks that arise in these activities are no different than those that arise in other bank products and business lines. However, these risk categories, including credit, interest rate, transaction, compliance, liquidity and reputation, often arise in ways that are more difficult to measure. As a result, activities such as derivatives and securitization activities require stronger risk management programs and managerial expertise than more traditional bank risk-taking activities.

The board is responsible for communicating its risk tolerance limits to management, making sure that management establishes control mechanisms that reflect that risk tolerance, reviewing risk reports, confirming compliance with policy limits, and determining that the bank uses these products for approved purposes.

1. Financial Derivatives

Financial derivatives derive their value from the performance of underlying interest rates, foreign exchange rates, equity prices, commodity prices, or credit quality. A bank can use derivatives to reduce business risks, expand product offerings to customers, trade for profit, manage capital and funding costs, and alter the risk-reward profile of a particular item or an entire balance sheet. As with all financial products, derivatives present risk, and directors should make sure that applicable risks are managed as part of the bank's overall risk management program. Because financial derivatives can be complicated instruments, directors must make sure that the bank has appropriate expertise to identify, measure, monitor and control the entire risk spectrum of all products used.[12]

Banks can execute derivative contracts either on an exchange or privately with a dealer. Exchange-traded contracts involve standardized terms; there is no negotiation of terms and conditions. Such contracts typically have excellent liquidity and readily observable market prices. The exchange is a counterparty to all contracts, which reduces credit risks. In contrast, banks negotiate the terms and conditions on transactions with dealers, and therefore can customize contract details, such as contract size and maturity date. Derivative contracts with dealers are referred to as "over the counter" (OTC) transactions because they do not occur on an exchange. These contracts are generally less liquid than exchange-traded contracts, and they do not have readily observable market prices. Most significantly, OTC contracts with dealers create credit risk for each party. As a result, banks participating in the OTC derivatives market should identify creditworthy counterparties, analyze the potential credit exposures of derivative transactions, and establish appropriate credit facilities.

Similar to other financial instruments, a derivative contract can gain and lose value. As a result, prior to entering into a derivatives transaction, management should understand the sensitivity of the value of that contract to changes in market factors, such as interest rates, that will determine its value.

A derivative contract's "current credit exposure" refers to the amount of money a counterparty would owe the bank if the two parties terminated the contract today. However, this current credit exposure is not a complete measure of credit risk. "Potential future exposure" refers to a statistical estimate of how large the current credit exposure on a derivative contract (or a portfolio of such contracts) could become over the life of the contract. It represents the amount of money the counterparty could owe the bank. The sum of current credit exposure and

---

[12] See the "Risk Management of Financial Derivatives" booklet of the *Comptroller's Handbook* for additional information on financial derivatives, available at www.occ.gov/static/publications/handbook/deriv.pdf.

potential future exposure is total credit exposure, the metric a bank should measure and manage.

Current credit exposure + Potential future exposure = Total credit exposure

When a bank enters into an OTC derivative transaction, the transaction should be priced so that it has no current credit exposure for either party. Such contracts are fairly priced. "Off market" contracts have initial value to one of the counterparties. They essentially represent an extension of credit. Off-market transactions deserve extra scrutiny because they are exceptions to normal business practices.

Parties to a derivatives contract often collateralize their exposures with high quality, liquid collateral to reduce credit exposures. Collateral reduces current credit exposure to a net current credit exposure, if the bank monitors the value of its derivative transactions and calls for the collateral when it needs to do so. Banks should establish policies that detail appropriate circumstances for pledging collateral to, and requiring it from, OTC counterparties.

Financial Accounting Standard 133 (FAS 133), "Accounting for Derivative Instruments and Hedging Activities," requires all derivative contracts to be on the balance sheet. The standard outlines broad categories of derivatives transactions: 1) fair value hedges; 2) cash flow hedges; 3) foreign exchange hedges; and 4) contracts not categorized as hedges.

Fair value hedges must be marked-to-market, with changes in value reflected in current earnings. Cash flow hedges must be marked-to-market, with changes in value reported directly in Other Comprehensive Income (OCI), the same category that includes unrealized gains and losses on available-for-sale securities. Foreign exchange hedges must be marked-to-market and treated as either a fair value or cash flow hedge, depending upon certain criteria. Derivative transactions that are not hedges must be marked-to-market, with any gain or loss reflected in current income.

The safe and sound use of derivatives is contingent upon the board ensuring that the bank has the relevant management expertise and overseeing and reviewing management's activities. Directors should use the following types of reports to assess financial derivatives activity:

- Credit Risk Exposures—identifies current credit exposure for each counterparty, which is the net value of all derivative contracts, assuming the bank has a legally enforceable netting agreement. The board should require management to obtain netting agreements since netting, like collateral, reduces credit risks. Such reports should also indicate credit limits and collateral requirements, as well as identify any credit concentrations.

- Trends in derivatives usage—tracks the notional amount of derivative contracts over time, by type of contract (futures, interest rate swaps, caps, floors, etc.) and by market risk factor (interest rates, equity prices, commodities, etc.).

- Compliance with policies and risk limits—details compliance with all board-approved derivative limits.

- Results of stress testing—augments the bank's risk measurement process by altering market variables to determine which scenarios may pose significant risk to the derivatives portfolio. Reports to the board should include the major assumptions used in each scenario. Stress testing is important for assessing both market and credit risk.

- Impact on income from derivatives—shows the accounting impact on the bank's income statement from its hedging and trading activities. In particular, such reports should assess whether the bank's hedging passes certain correlation requirements required by FAS 133 to measure hedge effectiveness and avoid having the entire contract marked-to-market through income.

Financial Derivatives Red Flags:

- Participation in transactions without appropriate knowledge of derivatives or experience in the market.

- Substantial exposure to a counterparty whose ongoing ability to meet its obligations is uncertain.

- Rapid growth in the notional amount of derivative contracts.

- A large ratio of derivative notional amounts to total assets.

- Written options on derivatives, such as interest rate caps or floors.

- Concentration of credit risks (total credit exposure) with a derivatives counterparty.

- Use of complex or illiquid derivative contracts.

- Derivatives embedded in cash market securities.

- "Off market" derivative contracts (e.g., a loan to or from a counterparty).

- Derivative contracts executed without an assessment of interest rate and/or credit risks.

- Large net payments or receipts of cash.

- Unilateral collateral posting (collateral arrangements should be bilateral).

- Use of only one firm for all, or nearly all, derivative transactions.

- Activity in new derivative products without subjecting the product to a new product review.

- Insufficient understanding of accounting rules for derivatives (FAS 133).

- Insufficient understanding of rules for derivative transactions with affiliates (12 CFR 223).

- Absence of legally enforceable netting agreements.

2. Asset Securitization

In asset securitization, interests in loans and other receivables are packaged, underwritten, and sold in the form of asset-backed securities. By using the securities markets to fund portions of the loan portfolio, banks can allocate capital more efficiently, access diverse and cost-effective funding sources, and better manage business risks. The board must determine whether the bank has the necessary resources and expertise to engage effectively in this business.

Although it is common for securitization transactions to receive substantial attention early in their tenure, the level of scrutiny generally declines over time. An effective board ensures that transactions are consistently and thoroughly supervised and monitored over the duration of the bank's involvement in these activities. Management reports to the board should include the performance of the underlying asset pools for all outstanding deals. Although the bank may have sold the ownership rights and control of the assets, its reputation as an underwriter or servicer remains exposed.[13]

The board of directors and bank management should ensure that:

- Independent risk management processes are in place to monitor securitization pool performance on an aggregate and individual transaction level. An effective risk management function includes appropriate information systems to monitor securitization activities.

- Management uses conservative valuation assumptions and modeling methodologies to establish, evaluate, and adjust the carrying value of retained interests on a regular and timely basis.

- Audit or internal review staffs periodically review data integrity, model algorithms, key underlying

---

[13] See the "Asset Securitization" booklet of the *Comptroller's Handbook* for additional information on asset securitization activities, available at www.occ.gov/static/publications/handbook/assetsec.pdf.

assumptions, and the appropriateness of the valuation and modeling process for the securitized assets retained by the institution. The findings of such reviews should be reported directly to the board or an appropriate board committee.

- Management maintains accurate and timely risk-based capital calculations, including recognition and reporting of any recourse obligation resulting from securitization activity.

- Internal limits are in place to govern the maximum amount of retained interests as a percentage of total equity capital.

- The institution has a realistic liquidity plan in place in case of market disruptions.

- Transactions do not create recourse to the bank.

- Reports to the board that monitor revolving transactions (credit cards, home equity lines, etc.) and installment loans, as appropriate:
  - The gross and net portfolio yield.
  - Delinquencies.
  - The charge-off rate.
  - The base rate (investor coupon plus servicing fees).
  - Monthly excess spread.
  - The rolling three-month average excess spread.
  - The monthly payment rate.
  - Principal prepayment speeds.
  - Outstanding principal compared with original security size.
  - Residuals.
  - Policy exceptions.
  - Covenant compliance.
  - Exposure limits by type of transaction and aggregate transactions outstanding.

Asset Securitization Red Flags:

- High level of residual assets relative to capital.

- Over-reliance on securitization as a funding source.

- Credit line increases without appropriate credit analysis.

- Increase in policy exceptions, scorecard overrides, or multiple reaging of delinquent accounts.

- Significant growth or pressure for growth.

- Shift in pricing and credit enhancement levels required by the market.

- Asset-backed securitization activities not fully integrated with critical bank planning processes.

- Adverse performance trends.

- Transactions with affiliates that are not at arm's length terms.

3. Credit Commitments

A formal loan commitment is a written agreement, signed by the borrower and lender, detailing terms and conditions under which the bank will lend a specified amount. The commitment has an expiration date. For agreeing to make the accommodation, the bank usually requires the prospective borrower to pay a fee, to put up a compensating balance, or both. A commitment can be irrevocable, as is a standby letter of credit facility, requiring the bank to lend when the customer calls upon it to do so. Or the commitment may be revocable, predicated upon the customer meeting certain covenants, often financial in nature.

The board should ensure that bank policy supports a loan officer's refusal to advance funds when a borrower is financially troubled, covenants have been broken, or other adverse conditions have arisen. The board should receive reports from management projecting the funding sources for loan commitments and lines of credits (based on the anticipated usage of such commitments and lines).

Credit Commitment Red Flags:

- Advancing funds to borrowers in financial difficulty, noncompliance with covenants, or other circumstances that make lending to them imprudent.

- Inadequate funding sources for anticipated use of loan commitments and lines of credit.

---

4. Mortgage Banking

Mortgage banking involves loan originations, purchases, and sales through the secondary mortgage market. A mortgage bank can retain or sell loans it originates and retain or sell the servicing on those loans. Through mortgage banking, national banks can participate in any or a combination of these activities.

The board should ensure that prudent risk management practices and controls are in place for its mortgage banking activities. The applicable risks associated with mortgage banking are credit, interest rate, price, transaction, liquidity, compliance, strategic, and reputation risks.[14]

When loans are sold into the secondary market, banks often retain the servicing and recognize mortgage servicing assets (MSAs), which are complex and volatile assets subject to interest rate risk. MSAs can become impaired when interest rates fall and borrowers refinance or prepay their mortgage loans. This impairment can lead to earnings volatility and erosion of capital, if the risks inherent in the MSAs have not been properly hedged.

The board of directors should ensure that the following key systems and controls are in place:

- Comprehensive documentation standards for all aspects of mortgage banking.

- MSA impairment analyses that use reasonable and supportable assumptions.

- Systems to measure and control interest rate risk.

- Accurate financial reporting systems, controls, and limits.

- Timely and accurate tracking of quality control exceptions.

- Appropriate tracking and collecting of required mortgage loan documents.

---

[14] See the "Mortgage Banking" booklet of the *Comptroller's Handbook* for additional information on mortgage banking, available at www.occ.gov/static/publications/handbook/mortgage.pdf.

- Appropriate monitoring and managing of risks associated with third-party originated loans.

- Adequate internal audit coverage.

The board should receive reports on:

- Internal audit, quality control, and compliance findings.

- Policy exceptions

- Valuation of MSAs.

- Hedged and un-hedged positions.

- Mark-to-market analyses.

- Profitability.

- Monthly production volume.

- Loan inventory aging.

- Delinquencies and foreclosures.

- Status of reserves.

- Operational efficiency.

Mortgage Banking Red Flags:

- High level of mortgage servicing assets relative to capital.

- Unsupported prepayment speeds, discount rates, and other assumptions in MSA valuation models.

- Rapid increases in mortgage loan production volume relative to the bank's capital or asset size without corresponding increases in staff or systems.

- Large gains or losses on the sale of mortgage loans.

- High or increasing level of third-party originated mortgage loans without proper controls.

- High or increasing level of policy exceptions.

- High or increasing volume of stale loans in mortgage inventory.

- High or increasing delinquency or foreclosure rates on serviced loans.

- Inadequate audit coverage of mortgage banking activities.

- Unauthorized exceptions to policy guidelines.

- Absence of meaningful risk limits.

G. Audits and Internal Control

Well-planned, properly structured, and effective audit and internal controls are essential to manage risk properly and to maintain a safe and sound bank. The board of directors must establish and maintain effective audit functions. An effective internal auditing process meets statutory and regulatory requirements[15] as well as other audit-related supervisory guidelines and standards. Directors cannot delegate their responsibility for oversight of the auditing function. However, they may delegate the design, implementation, and monitoring of specific internal controls to management and the testing and assessment of internal controls to others.

The internal control system should, with reasonable assurance, help prevent or detect inaccurate, incomplete, or unauthorized transactions; deficiencies in the safeguarding of assets; unreliable financial and regulatory reporting; violations of laws or regulations; and deviations from the institution's own policies and procedures. Both internal and external auditors should monitor and evaluate the effectiveness of internal controls. The board of directors should determine how intensive auditing must be to test and monitor internal controls effectively and to ensure the reliability of the bank's financial statements and reporting.

The board of directors should consider whether the bank's control systems and auditing methods, records, and procedures are proper in relation to the bank's:

- Size.

- Organization and ownership characteristics.

- Business activities and product lines.

- Operational diversity and complexity.

- Risk profile.

---

[15] Refer to "Internal and External Audits" booklet of the *Comptroller's Handbook* for additional information about the requirements of the Sarbanes-Oxley Act and other laws and regulations that affect audit functions. These booklets are available at www.occ.gov/static/publications/internal-external-audits.zip.

- Methods of processing data.

- Applicable legal and regulatory requirements.

The board of directors, or its audit committee, should meet regularly (at least quarterly) with the bank's internal auditor and review information on matters pertaining to the effectiveness of control systems and risk management processes and progress toward achieving the bank's overall audit objectives. Executive summary reports, or audit information packages, should be a part of these reviews and should include:

- Status reports on meeting the annual audit plan or schedule, including any adjustments to the plan or schedule, and activity reports on audits completed, in process, and deferred or cancelled.

- Information about audit staffing, independence, and training.

- Discussion of significant accounting issues or regulatory issuances pertaining to audit or controls.

- Copies of individual audit reports issued during the quarter or summaries of audits conducted and significant issues noted.

- Summaries of information technology, fiduciary, and consumer compliance audits, as warranted.

- Risk assessments performed or summaries thereof.

- Significant outstanding audit and control issues, in the form of tracking reports that describe the issues, when the issues were discovered, the person responsible for corrective action, the promised date of correction, and status of corrective action.

Audits and Internal Control Red Flags:

- Internal audit staff reporting to other than the board of directors or its audit committee.

- Any indications that management is trying to control or inhibit communications from internal audit staff to the board of directors.

- Unexplained or unexpected changes in external auditor or significant changes in the audit program.

- A reduction of, or increased turnover in, internal audit staff.

- A significant decrease in the audit budget.

- Internal or external auditors relying heavily on the other's conclusions.

- Employees in key or influential positions who were not on vacation or otherwise absent for two consecutive weeks during the year.

- Audit reports that do not address identified internal control weaknesses.

- Significant internal control or other deficiencies noted in audit reports that have not been corrected.

- The inability of management to provide timely and accurate financial, operational, and regulatory reports.

- Unreconciled differences between trial balances, subsidiary ledgers, and the general ledger.

- A qualified, adverse, or disclaimer opinion from an external auditor.

- An external auditor or audit firm that has a financial interest in the bank, loan from the bank, or other conflict of interest.

- An external auditor or audit firm that performs both financial statement audit services and other non-audit services, including outsourced internal audit services, for the bank.

- An external audit lead audit partner who has performed external audit services for the bank for more than five consecutive years.

- Internal audit not meeting the audit schedule, or not adequately covering significant risk areas.

H. Consumer Compliance

Compliance with consumer laws and regulations is an integral part of a bank's business strategy. Violations and noncompliance can significantly impair a bank's reputation, value, earning ability, and business opportunity. To effectively monitor compliance with consumer laws and regulations, the board must receive timely and accurate reports on compliance matters. To ensure that directors learn immediately about significant violations and noncompliance, the designated compliance officer

Consumer Compliance Red Flags:

- Lack of periodic reports to the board on compliance matters.

- The compliance officer reporting to someone other than the board of directors or a committee of the board.

- Significant deficiencies identified in compliance reviews that have not been corrected in a timely manner.

- Significant turnover, including the compliance officer, or a reduction in the staff responsible for ensuring compliance with laws or specific consumer products.

- Lack of evidence that compliance was adequately considered when new products and delivery systems were developed and introduced, or when new marketing materials were designed.

should have direct access to the board. The board should periodically receive formal reports on compliance matters. The complexity and extent of reporting will vary with the complexity and extent of the bank's operations, products, services, customers, and geographies served.

Although compliance with all consumer laws and regulations should be important to all boards of directors, boards often place special emphasis on fair lending, the Community Reinvestment Act (CRA), and the Bank Secrecy Act (BSA).[16]

- A significant increase in customer dissatisfaction and complaints (either received directly or sent to the OCC).[17]

- Significant deviation from policy or operational standards.

- Inadequate review of the compliance function by internal audit.

- Lack of evidence that bank employees are receiving current and adequate compliance training appropriate for their positions and responsibilities.

- Lack of due diligence when the bank purchases compliance third-party vendor services and products.

- Rapid or significant growth in a product line.

[16] Refer to the "Bank Secrecy Act/Anti-Money Laundering;" "Compliance Management Systems;" "Fair Lending Examination Procedures;" "Overview;" and "Community Reinvestment Act Examination Procedures" booklets of the *Comptroller's Handbook* for additional information on these compliance areas. These handbooks are available at www.occ.treas.gov/publications/publications-by-type/comptrollers-handbook/index-comptrollers-handbook.html.

[17] Contact the OCC's Customer Assistance Group to obtain information about consumer compliance related complaints. Contact information:1-800-613-6743 or customer.assistance@occ.treas.gov.

1. Fair Lending

Fair lending is making credit available in accordance with the requirements of the Fair Housing Act, the Equal Credit Opportunity Act, and Regulation B. Compliance can be achieved merely by establishing prudent lending practices and by treating customers consistently. These practices include establishing clear standards and procedures for credit decisions, setting reasonable limits on discretion by lending personnel, and maintaining appropriate documentation.

Fair Lending Red Flags:

- An existing or proposed lending policy that includes, directly or indirectly, reference to any prohibited basis (race, color, national origin, religion, sex, age, marital status, familial status, handicap, receipt of public assistance, or the exercise of a right under the Consumer Credit Protection Act).

- An existing or proposed lending policy whose standards for underwriting, pricing, or setting terms and conditions are vague or unduly subjective, or which allow substantial loan officer discretion.

- Any statements by officers, employees, or agents, indicating a preference, prejudice, or stereotyping on a prohibited basis, or an aversion to doing business in minority areas.

- Segmentation of product markets, advertisements, promotions, application channels, or other access to credit along the lines of racial or national origin characteristics of applicants or geographic areas.

- Consumer complaints alleging discrimination in specific transactions.

- Substantially fewer loans originated in areas with relatively high concentrations of minority group residents than in areas with comparable income levels, but relatively low concentrations of minority residents.

- Disparities in Home Mortgage Disclosure Act (HMDA) data.

- Low levels of minority applicants even though minorities represent a significant part of the service area.

- Use of credit scoring models that have not been validated.

2. Community Reinvestment Act

The Community Reinvestment Act (CRA) encourages national banks to help meet the credit needs of their entire communities. While the regulation no longer requires directors to document how actively they participate in community groups or civic organizations, the entire board's attention, leadership, and commitment are essential to successful CRA performance. Although the bank is not required to assess its CRA progress, periodic self-assessments can help the board determine the bank's progress toward achieving its internal CRA goals and performance objectives.

CRA Red Flags:

- Substantial disparities in the numbers of loans originated within groups of contiguous low- or moderate-income geographies.

- Reports that show lending performance, particularly when viewed against primary competitors, are significantly below the performance of other lenders in the bank's assessment area.

- Reports that show that the bank has few or no qualified investments in its assessment area, even though investment opportunities exist.

- Customer complaints about the level of services and products offered in some parts of the bank's trade area compared with those offered in other areas served by the bank.

- Substantial errors in CRA and HMDA data and requests for data resubmission.

---

3. Bank Secrecy Act/Anti-Money Laundering (AML)

The Bank Secrecy Act (BSA) and related regulations require that the board of directors approve a written program for compliance with the BSA. Compliance with BSA is an important part of the bank's operations. Noncompliance can result in serious harm to the bank's reputation and in the assessment of penalties.

The board should ensure that the bank's program for BSA includes proper internal controls, independent testing, appropriate staff training, and updates whenever regulatory changes take place. The bank's audit program should confirm that controls are adequate, that appropriate currency transaction reports (CTRs) and suspicious activity reports (SARs) are filed, that the directors are informed about any SAR filings, and a customer identification program is implemented. The board designates a person who is responsible for coordinating and monitoring day-to-day compliance.

Specifically, directors should ensure that the BSA compliance program includes appropriate account opening and customer identification verification procedures, determine the nature and purpose of the account, and identify the bank's services or products the customer will use. Additionally the BSA program should include monitoring systems and procedures to ensure that the bank is aware of any suspicious activities.

Directors and bank management must be particularly alert to the following potentially high-risk accounts, services, and geographic areas:

- High-risk accounts—accounts held by currency exchangers and dealers, money transmitters, businesses engaged in check-cashing, casinos, car or boat dealerships, travel agencies, non-governmental organizations and charities, senior foreign political persons, and entities from foreign countries known as drug trafficking or money-laundering havens. High volumes of cash, wire transfers, or official checks are also indicators of high-risk accounts.

- High-risk services and products—include private banking, payable through accounts, personal investment companies, offshore accounts, international correspondent accounts, international pouch activity, and international wires.

- High-risk geographic locations— include:
    - Areas known as drug trafficking, money-laundering, or tax havens.
    - Jurisdictions identified by intergovernmental organizations as noncooperative with global anti-money laundering efforts.
    - Jurisdictions identified by the Secretary of the Treasury as being of money laundering concern, or identified as sympathizing with terrorist efforts, and jurisdictions designated by the U. S. government as sponsoring terrorism.

BSA Red Flags:

- Audit is not risk focused.

- Audit does not test for suspicious activity.

- Bank personnel are not trained regularly on the BSA and how to identify possible suspicious activity.

- Correspondence is received from the Internal Revenue Service that indicates the bank is filing incomplete or incorrect currency transaction reports.

- The volume of SARs or CTRs is very high or very low.

- The bank acquires large deposit relationships, but management is unfamiliar with the depositor's business or line of work.

- Account activity is inconsistent with the known business of the account holder.

- Customers use an unusually large volume of wires, official checks, money orders, or traveler's checks, especially to or from a high-risk geographical area.

- Bank customers route funds through multiple foreign or domestic banks or wire funds in and out within a short period.

- Customers have multiple accounts for no apparent reason or make frequent transfers between accounts either within or outside the bank.

- Customers have an unusually large volume of cash or use a disproportionate amount of cash versus checks.

- Accounts have dramatic changes or spikes in activity or in the volume of money flowing through the account.

- Customer asks that their transactions be exempted from CTR reporting requirements, or that the CTR not be filed, or makes cash deposits just under the CTR reporting threshold.

- Transactions to or from entities or high-risk geographic locations that do not comport with the customer's known business operations.

I. Asset Management

Asset management activities include fiduciary services, investment advisory services, brokerage, investment company services, securities custody, and securities processing services. These services may be provided in a centralized division of the bank, through different divisions in different geographical locations, in bank operating subsidiaries, bank affiliates, and through arrangements with unaffiliated third parties. National banks offer these services to maintain competitiveness, meet customer demand, and enhance fee income. In many banks, asset management revenue is a significant contributor to total income and profitability.[18]

National banks that provide asset management services operate in a broad and complex risk environment and should identify and control the risks associated with the products and services they provide. Consequently, board oversight of asset management-related activities is essential to effective management of these services. Although the board may assign functions related to the exercise of fiduciary powers to any director, officer, or employee of the bank, the board is ultimately responsible for any financial loss or reduction in shareholder value suffered by the bank.

An effective board of directors will oversee the development of asset management-related risk limits, approve new products or services, and monitor on-going business plans. Boards of directors should expect to see routinely financial performance reports related to each asset management business.

Directors generally find the following reports helpful in assessing the risks and financial performance of asset management activities:

- New business/lost business reports—identify key characteristics of new clients and provide information on closed accounts. Directors should be aware of potential systemic reasons for account closings, including customer

---

[18] Refer to the "Asset Management" booklet of the *Comptroller's Handbook* for additional information on asset management, available at www.occ.gov/static/publications/handbook/assetmgmt.pdf.

service problems, product deficiencies (including sub par performance), mishandling of accounts, and operational errors.

- Investment reports—provide information on investments purchased and sold for accounts and the strategy underlying those investment decisions.

- Investment performance analyses—provide information about the performance of the investment advisory and fiduciary portfolios and should compare that performance with applicable indices.

- Litigation reports—summarize the volume, potential dollar exposure, and nature of pending or threatened litigation. These reports should provide current information on the status of existing litigation and should be reviewed by the bank's legal counsel.

- Profitability/budget reports—may capture information by product line, by business unit, or for asset management activities as a whole. The supporting information should enable directors to evaluate the success of business strategies as well as management's performance.

- Trust bank capital and liquidity analysis reports—evaluate factors, such as the composition, stability, and direction of revenue; the level and composition of expenses in relation to the bank's operations; the level of earnings retention; the bank's liquidity position and management's ability to control it; the volume, type, and growth in managed and non-managed assets; the quantity and direction of reputation and strategic risk; the quality of risk management processes, including the adequacy of internal and external audit, internal controls, and the compliance management system; and the impact of external factors, including economic conditions, competition, technology enhancements, legislative changes, and precedent-setting court decisions.

- Fiduciary audit reports—contain conclusions on the effectiveness of the bank's internal controls and operating practices. Reports are usually separate audit reports and are required by 12 CFR 9.9.

Asset Management Red Flags:

- Unanticipated or unexplained changes in business strategies.

- Substantial changes or growth in account types, account balances, or products and services offered.

- The existence of accounts with unusually high cash balances or large extended overdrafts.

- Accounts that are closed shortly after being opened and funded.

- High volumes of exchanged annuities, switched mutual funds, or early redemptions of retail brokerage investments.

- Purchases or sales of securities held in a fiduciary capacity through a retail brokerage unit that were not previously approved by the board or investment committee.

- Fiduciary assets or relationships of a kind the bank lacks expertise to manage (e.g., mineral interests or farm/ranch properties).

- Unresolved significant audit and compliance findings.

- Significant levels of documentation deficiencies and policy exceptions, including exceptions to account and business acceptance policies.

- Unexplained or frequent changes in vendors, service providers, or auditors.

- Significant outsourcing of services without management oversight and control.

- Purchase or sale of assets between fiduciary accounts and the bank or bank insiders.

- Sale, loan, or transfer of fiduciary account assets to the bank or bank insiders.

J. Management Information Systems

Many of a bank's business decisions are predicated on the sophistication and reliability of information systems. For example, many banks must choose to either forgo offering certain new products or go to the expense of upgrading their information systems needed to support those new products. Software and telecommunications, data processing, computer networks, and the Internet are all possible components of a bank's information system.

The board should ensure that the bank has an adequate business continuity plan. Operating disruptions can occur with or without warning, and the results may be predictable or unknown. Effective business continuity planning establishes the basis for financial institutions to maintain and recover business processes when operations have been disrupted unexpectedly. The objectives of a business continuity plan are to minimize financial loss to the institution, continue to serve customers and financial market participants, and mitigate the negative effects disruptions can have on an institution's strategic plans, reputation, operations, liquidity, credit quality, market position, and ability to comply with applicable laws and regulations.

The board should also ensure that the bank has appropriate policies, procedures, and controls in place to ensure that data systems have adequate safeguards to protect sensitive financial data and customer information and that key systems can be restored or accessed in the event of an emergency or a disaster. Because technological advancements are increasingly changing the character of day-to-day banking activities, board members should learn as much as possible about their bank's information system, and should be aware of any needed or proposed changes to the system and how those changes may affect security.

A bank's information system architecture has two major functions: processing bank transactions and supplying reports to management and the board about managing business risk. The management information system (MIS) supplies these reports. One of MIS's most important functions is to help management assess the bank's risks. Management decisions based on ineffective, inaccurate, or incomplete MIS may increase risk in all areas.

Not all of a bank's transactions are processed inside the bank. Many vendors can be essential to the processing of bank transactions. If vendors play important roles in the bank's information system, the board must ensure that the vendor's services and reports meet the same standards as those generated within the bank.

To assess a bank's information systems, the board must consider whether the MIS process provides the information necessary to manage the organization effectively. A reliable MIS ensures that the bank maintains basic control over financial record keeping. The MIS also should support the institution's longer term strategic goals and objectives.

The following characteristics of a management information system help to ensure prompt and well-informed decision-making:

- Timeliness—The system should expedite the reporting of information. The system should promptly collect and edit data, summarize results, and correct errors.

- Accuracy—A reliable system of automated and manual internal controls must exist for all information system processing activities. Information should receive appropriate editing, balancing, and internal control checks.

- Security and Integrity —The system should not be subject to unauthorized changes in or access to important data.

- Consistency—Consistency in how data are collected and reported is extremely important. Differences in these activities can distort trend analysis and information reported to the board.

- Completeness—Decision-makers must require complete information in a summarized form. Reports should be designed to eliminate clutter and voluminous detail, thereby avoiding information overload.

- Relevance—MIS information is relevant if needed by the board, executive management, and the bank's operational areas.

Management Information Systems Red Flags:

- MIS systems that result in unauthorized disclosure of customer information and/or lapses of security in protecting customer information.

- MIS systems that fail to keep pace with or prove unreliable in the face of existing or new business lines.

- Systems problems attributed to integration of systems; e.g., in conjunction with an acquisition.

- MIS reports reflecting problems relating to vendor management or outsourcing arrangements.

- Increasing levels of fraud loss.

- Lack of an adequate business continuity plan.

- An information technology system that cannot be described readily by appropriate management. Management is unable to provide a basic diagram of the system architecture or a comprehensive list of service providers.

- MIS reports that are untimely, incomplete, or inaccurate.

- MIS reports that lack relevance or are too detailed for use as an effective decision-making tool.

- Inconsistency of information contained within MIS reports.

- A lack of system audits or unresolved audit deficiencies.

K. Internet Banking

Internet banking refers to systems that provide access to accounts and general information on bank products and services through a personal computer or other intelligent device. Internet banking products and services can include wholesale, retail, and fiduciary products. Ultimately, the products and services obtained through Internet banking may mirror products and services offered through other bank delivery channels.[19]

Banks typically make their decisions to offer Internet banking based on competition, cost efficiencies, geographical reach, branding, and customer demographics issues. Two basic kinds of Internet banking Web sites are being employed in the marketplace.

- Informational— Provides access to general information about the institution and its products and services.

- Transactional—Allows customers to execute transactions.

Internet banking, and particularly transactional sites, create new risk control challenges for banks. The board should ensure that management possesses the knowledge and skills to manage the bank's use of Internet banking technology and technology-related risks. Management must implement a system of internal controls commensurate with the bank's level of risk. The board reviews, approves, and monitors Internet banking technology-related projects. They determine whether the technology and products are in line with the bank's strategic goals and meet a need in their market. The board receives regular reports on the technologies employed, the risks assumed, and how those risks are managed.

To achieve a high level of confidence with consumers and businesses, the Internet banking system must be secure. Key

---

[19] Refer to the *Federal Financial Institutions Examination Council (FFIEC) Information Technology Examination Handbook* (IT InfoBase) at www.ffiec.gov/ffiecinfobase/html_pages/it_01.htm for more information on electronic banking.

components of a system that will help maintain a high level of public confidence in an open network environment include:

- Security—The level of logical and physical security must be commensurate with the sensitivity of the information and the individual bank's risk tolerance.

- Authentication—Customers, banks, and merchants need assurances that they know the identity of the persons with whom they are dealing.

- Trust—Customers need to know that they are dealing with the bank and not some fraudulent or "spoofed" Web site. A trusted third party, or certificate authority, is used to verify identities in cyberspace. Digital certificates may play an important role in authenticating parties and thus establishing trust in Internet banking systems.

- Nonrepudiation—The undeniable proof of participation by both the sender and receiver in a transaction is important. Public key encryption technology was developed to deal with this issue.

- Privacy—Concerns over the proper collection and use of personal information are likely to increase with the continued growth of electronic commerce and the Internet. Banks should recognize and respond proactively to privacy issues.

- Availability—Users of electronic commerce capabilities expect access to networks 24 hours per day, seven days per week.

Internet Banking Red Flags:

- A system that does not have regular reviews and certifications by independent auditors, consultants, or technology experts.

- Unresolved or repeat audit deficiencies.

- Management that is unable to provide a basic description of the system architecture, a comprehensive inventory of service providers, or effective vendor management.

- Systems, products, or services are inconsistent with the bank's strategic plan.

- Systems without contingency and business resumption plans, or with a low level of operational reliability.

- Web sites that do not meet customers' needs for information security and privacy, and those without effective customer authentication.

- No evidence that the bank's compliance officer reviewed information prior to distribution on the Web site.

L. OCC's Overall Assessment

The board of directors must review the OCC's report of examination to obtain the OCC's objective assessment of the bank. The report of examination findings address the bank's safety and soundness, the quantity of risk, the quality of risk management, the level of supervisory concern, and the direction of risk. The board should pay particular attention to weaknesses and adverse trends identified during the examination and to the actions management plans to take or have already taken to address those weaknesses. These topics are generally addressed in the "Matters Requiring Attention" and "Overall Conclusions" sections of the report of examination.

1. Ratings

The OCC and other federal bank and thrift regulatory agencies use the Uniform Financial Institutions Rating System (UFIRS) to assign composite and component ratings to an institution. This system is a general framework for uniformly evaluating the safety and soundness of banks. The UFIRS, also know as the CAMELS rating system, provides a point-in-time assessment of a bank's current performance, financial condition, compliance with laws and regulations, management ability, and overall operational soundness.

A bank's CAMELS composite rating integrates ratings in six component areas: the adequacy of capital (C), the quality of assets (A), the capability of management (M), the quality and level of earnings (E), the adequacy of liquidity (L), and the sensitivity to market risk (S). Ratings are also assigned for the specialty areas of information technology, trust, consumer compliance, and compliance with the Community Reinvestment Act.

Composite and component ratings range from "1" to "5", with the exception of CRA which has four composite rating categories. A "1" is the highest and best rating, indicating the strongest performance and the best risk management practices relative to the institution's size, complexity, and risk profile. A bank rated "1" poses the least supervisory concern. A "5" rating is the lowest and worst rating, indicating the most critically deficient level of performance and inadequate risk management practices relative to the institution's size, complexity, and risk profile. A bank rated "5" is at risk of failing and poses the greatest supervisory concern.

2. Risk Assessment System (RAS)

The RAS is a method of identifying, evaluating, documenting, and communicating OCC's assessment of the quantity of risk, the quality of risk management, and the direction of risk at each bank. This assessment takes both a current and a prospective view of the institution's risk profile. The OCC has defined nine risk categories: credit, interest rate, liquidity, price, foreign currency translation, transaction, compliance, strategic, and reputation. For the first seven risk categories, the OCC makes the following assessments:

- Quantity of risk is the level or volume of risk that exists and is characterized as low, moderate, or high.

- Quality of risk management is how well risks are identified, measured, controlled, and monitored and is characterized as strong, satisfactory, or weak.

- Aggregate risk is a summary judgment about the level of supervisory concern; it incorporates judgments about the quantity of risk and the quality of risk management (examiners weigh the relative importance of each). Aggregate risk is characterized as low, moderate, or high.

- Direction of risk is the probable change in the bank's risk profile over the next 12 months and is characterized as decreasing, stable, or increasing. The direction of risk often influences the OCC's supervisory strategy, including how much validation is needed. If the risk is decreasing, the examiner expects, based on current information, aggregate risk to decline over the next 12 months. If the risk is stable, the examiner expects aggregate risk to remain unchanged. If the risk is increasing, the examiner expects aggregate risk to be higher in 12 months.

The other two categories of risk, strategic and reputation, are less quantifiable than the first seven. Although these two risks affect the bank's franchise value, they cannot be measured precisely. Consequently, the OCC has a modified risk assessment and measuring process for them. This process includes assessing aggregate risk and direction of risk.

3. Relationship of RAS and Uniform Ratings

The risk assessment system and the uniform interagency rating systems are distinct yet closely related evaluation methods used by the OCC during its supervisory process. Both provide information about a bank's overall soundness, financial and operational weaknesses or adverse trends, problems or deteriorating conditions, and risk management practices.

The major distinction between the RAS and the CAMELS rating systems is the prospective nature of the RAS. The CAMELS rating system primarily provides a point-in-time assessment of an institution's current performance. The RAS reflects an examiner's judgment about current and future quantity of risk, quality of risk management, and direction of risk in each bank.

Still, because of their related characteristics, the risk assessment system and the ratings systems affect one another. For example, examiners may rate aggregate and direction of credit risk in a bank with increasing adverse trends and weak risk management practices as "moderate and increasing" or "high and increasing." This risk assessment may influence downward the CAMELS component rating for asset quality, if the current rating does not reflect the appropriate supervisory concern. When the two methods are used in this manner, they provide an important verification of supervisory findings and planned activities.

Overall Assessment Red Flags:

- A composite, component, or specialty rating that is lower than in previous examinations. Directors should be particularly concerned about ratings of 3, 4, and 5.

- A risk category that is rated moderate and increasing, or high.

- A risk category in which the direction of risk is rated as increasing.

- A risk category in which the quantity of risk is moderate or high, and the quality of risk management is rated as weak.

- A risk category in which the rating is inconsistent with the risk tolerance of the bank.

- "Matters Requiring Attention" or items of concern in the "Overall Conclusions" section of the report of examination.

- Many or repetitive violations of law.

- High or increasing level of classified assets.

- Reference to noncompliance with bank policy or recurring internal control deficiencies.

- Reference to an activity for which directors may be liable or subject to civil money penalties.

- Reference to noncompliance with one of the OCC's administrative actions (cease-and-desist order, formal agreement, memorandum of understanding, or commitment letter).

III. Problem Banks and Bank Failure

To gain a better understanding of why banks fail, the OCC studied selected national banks that failed during the 1980s. The study showed that while poor economic conditions make it more difficult for a bank to steer a profitable course, the policies and procedures adopted by the board of directors have a greater influence on whether a bank will succeed or fail. Improperly functioning boards of directors and management were the primary internal cause of problem and failed banks. The quality of a bank's board and management depends on the experience, capability, judgment, and integrity of its directors and senior officers. Common oversight or management deficiencies identified in failed banks are listed below.

- Uninformed or inattentive board of directors.

  - Nonexistent or poorly followed loan policies.

  - Inadequate systems to ensure compliance with policies or law.

  - Inadequate controls or supervision of key bank officers or departments.

  - Inadequate problem identification systems.

  - Decisions made by one dominant person.

  - Poor judgment in the decision-making process.

- Negative influence from insiders.

  - Lack of policies or inadequate audits, controls, and systems.

  - Insiders of poor integrity.

- Overly aggressive activity by board or management.

  - Liberal lending policies.

  - Excessive loan growth compared with management or staff abilities, cost systems, or funding sources.

- Undue reliance on volatile liabilities.
- Inadequate liquid assets/secondary source of liquidity.

- Other.
  - Excessive credit exceptions.
  - Over lending.
  - Collateral-based lending and insufficient cash-flow analysis.
  - An emphasis on earnings over sound policies, procedures and controls.
  - Inadequate due diligence when acquiring a business, such as a mortgage lender.
  - Failure to establish adequate policies, procedures and controls before entering into a new business (i.e., credit cards and payday lending).
  - Unwarranted concentrations of credit.

List of OCC References

A User's Guide for the Uniform Bank Performance Report
(http://www.ffiec.gov/UBPR.htm)

An Examiner's Guide to Investment Products and Practices

*An Examiner's Guide to Problem Bank Identification,
Rehabilitation, and Resolution*

FFIEC Information Technology Examination Handbook
(IT InfoBase) (www.ffiec.gov/ffiecinfobase/html_pages/it_01.
html)

Money Laundering: A Banker's Guide to Avoiding Problems

The Director's Book: The Role of a National Bank Director

Booklets in the *Comptroller's Handbook* series:

"Allowance for Loan and Lease Losses"

"Asset Securitization"

"Bank Supervision Process"

"Community Bank Supervision"

"Insider Activities"

"Interest Rate Risk"

"Internal and External Audits"

"Internal Control"

"Large Bank Supervision"

"Liquidity"

"Loan Portfolio Management"

"Management Information Systems"

"Mortgage Banking"

"Risk Management of Financial Derivatives"

Booklets in the *Comptroller's Handbook for Asset Management* series:

"Asset Management"

"Conflicts of Interest"

"Custody Services"

"Investment Management Services"

"Personal Fiduciary Services"

Booklets in the *Comptroller's Handbook for Consumer Compliance* series:

"Bank Secrecy Act / Anti-Money Laundering"

"Community Reinvestment Act Examination Procedures"

"Compliance Management Systems"

"Fair Lending"

"Overview"

OCC Advisory Letters:

Advisory Letter 2001-5, "Brokered and Rate-Sensitive Deposits," May 11, 2001

Advisory Letter 2003-2, "Guidelines for National Banks to Guard against Predatory and Abusive Lending Practices," February 21, 2003

Advisory Letter 2003-3, "Avoiding Predatory and Abusive Lending Practices in Brokered and Purchased Loans," February 21, 2003

OCC Bulletins:

OCC Bulletin 96-25, "Fiduciary Risk Management of Derivatives and Mortgage-backed Securities," April 30, 1996

OCC Bulletin 97-1, "Uniform Financial Institutions Rating System and Disclosure of Component Ratings: Message to Bankers and Examiners," January 3, 1997

OCC Bulletin 97-14, "Uniform Financial Institutions Rating System and Disclosure of Component Ratings: Questions and Answers," March 7, 1997

OCC Bulletin 98-3, "Technology Risk Management: Guidance for Bankers and Examiners," February 4, 1998

OCC Bulletin 98-20, "Investment Securities: Policy Statement," April 27, 1998

OCC Bulletin 99-3, "Uniform Rating System for Information Technology: Message to Bankers and Examiners," January 29, 1999

OCC Bulletin 99-37, "Interagency Policy Statement on External Auditing Programs: External Audit," October 7, 1999

OCC Bulletin 99-46, "Interagency Guidance on Asset Securitization Activities: Asset Securitization," December 14, 1999

OCC Bulletin 2000-16, "Risk Modeling: Model Validation," May 30, 2000

OCC Bulletin 2000-23, "Bank Purchases of Life Insurance: Guidelines for National Banks," July 20, 2000

OCC Bulletin 2000-26, "Supervision of National Trust Banks: Capital and Liquidity," September 28, 2000

OCC Bulletin 2001-17, "Uniform Rating System for Information Technology, Change in URSIT Usage for Examinations of National Banks," April 6, 2001

OCC Bulletin 2001-47, "Third-Party Relationships: Risk Management Principles," November 1, 2001

OCC Bulletin 2002-17, "Accrued Interest Receivable: Regulatory Capital and Accrued Interest Receivable Assets," May 17, 2002

OCC Bulletin 2002-19, "Unsafe and Unsound Investment Portfolio Practices: Supplemental Guidance," May 22, 2002

OCC Bulletin 2002-20, "Implicit Recourse in Asset Securitization: Policy Implementation," May 23, 2002

OCC Bulletin 2002-21, "Covenants Tied to Supervisory Actions in Securitization Documents: Interagency Guidance," May 23, 2002

OCC Bulletin 2002-22, "Capital Treatment of Recourse, Direct Credit Substitutes, and Residual Interests in Asset Securitizations: Interpretations of Final Rule," May 23, 2002

OCC Bulletin 2002-39, "Investment Portfolio Credit Risks: Safekeeping Arrangements: Supplemental Guidance," September 5, 2002

OCC Bulletin 2002-45, "Accrued Interest Receivable: Accounting for the Accrued Interest Receivable Asset," December 4, 2002

OCC Bulletin 2003-9, "Mortgage Banking: Interagency Advisory on Mortgage Banking," February 25, 2003

OCC Bulletin 2003-12, "Interagency Policy Statement on Internal Audit and Internal Audit Outsourcing: Revised Guidance on Internal Audit and its Outsourcing," March 17, 2003

These publications are available on the Web at www.occ.gov (under Publications or News and Issuances).

www.ingramcontent.com/pod-product-compliance
Lightning Source LLC
Chambersburg PA
CBHW080515290526
45790CB00006B/2170